101 Uses For A Dachshund

WILLOW CREEK PRESS

Published by Willow Creek Press, Inc.
P.O. Box 147, Minocqua, Wisconsin 54548

Design: Donnie Rubo
Printed in China

Bedmate

Playmate

Exercise partner

Washcloth

Car security system

Backseat driver

Detective

Monument

Security
guard

Security alarm

Lawn ornament

A friend that is a good listener...

...and will never leave your side.

Bed warmer

Foot warmer   Leg warmer

Garbage disposal

Moist towelette

Sprinkler

Gardener

Lawn fertilizer

Birdwatcher

Palm reader

Dreamcatcher

Curiosity seeker

Wind up toy

Someone who looks up to you...

...and waits for you.

Protagonist

Antagonist

Hugger   Kisser

Secret admirer

Snowplow

Shovel

Someone that
looks out for you...

...and always has your back.

Guard   Greeter

Doormen

Dog trainer

Horse whisperer

Someone that makes sure
your coffee isn't too hot.

And will always share
a drink with you.

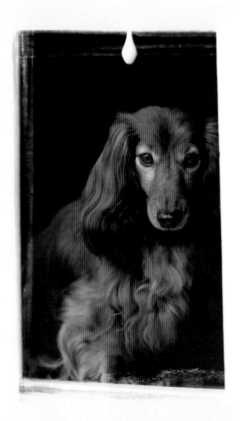

Suncatcher

Wind vane

Landscaper

Florist

Logger

Lifeguard

Electrician

Chauffeur

Dental hygenist

Scholar

Archeologist

Table busser

Dishwasher

Seamstress

Cobbler

Fireman

Plumber

Photographer

Sculptor

T.V. technician

IT specialist

Comedian

Clown

Interior Decorator

Mover

Carpenter

Babysitter

Wrestler

Explorer

Christmas gift

Elf   Santa Claus

Nutcracker

Attack dog

Musician

Recording artist

Olympic sprinter

High jumper   Hurdler

Mountain climber

Backpacker

Beach bum

Trendsetter

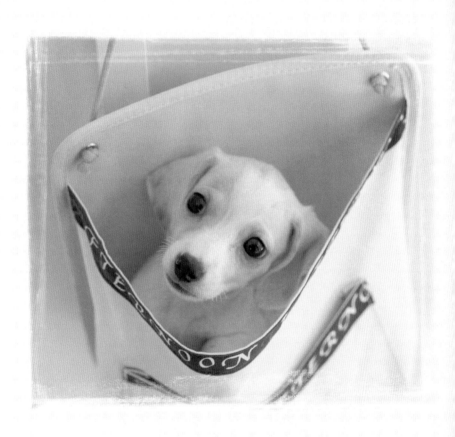

Stowaway

Luggage

Fashion accessory

Fashionista

Taste tester

Food critic

Hipster

Diva

Party
animal

Sommelier

Soccer player

Vice grips

Trailblazer

Best friend